Journal for the Journey

The Companion to
A Woman's Journey to
the Heart of God

Cynthia Heald

OLIVER
NELSON

THOMAS NELSON PUBLISHERS
Nashville • Atlanta • London • Vancouver

Published in Nashville, Tennessee, by Thomas Nelson, Inc., Publishers, and distributed in Canada by Word Communications, Ltd., Richmond, British Columbia.

Published in association with the literary agency of Alive Communications, 1465 Kelly Johnson Blvd., Suite #320, Colorado Springs, CO 80920.

Scripture quotations noted *The Message* are from *The Message: The New Testament in Contemporary English*. Copyright © 1993 by Eugene H. Peterson.

Scripture quotations noted NLT are taken from the *Holy Bible,* New Living Translation, copyright © 1996. Used by permission of Tyndale House Publishers, Inc., Wheaton, Illinois 60189. All rights reserved.

ISBN 0-7852-7126-0

Printed in the United States of America.

1 2 3 4 5 6 — 02 01 00 99 98 97

Contents

Preface

Whenever I read a book, I want to either make notes in the margins or write down a particular truth that I want to remember and think about. Most often, there is not enough space to write in the book, and I never seem to have a notebook or paper with me when I'm reading. That is why I am excited about this *Journal for the Journey*. It is an ideal complement to the book *A Woman's Journey to the Heart of God*.

Morton T. Kelsey writes, "The journal not only gives us a safe way of dealing with the feelings that are often ready to burst out of us, but offers us objectivity about them as well."* I hope that as you read *A Woman's Journey to the Heart of God*, you will be challenged to meditate on your views of God or on decisions you might need to make along your journey to God's heart.

My prayer is that your life will be changed as you write about and pray over your life as God's child. My desire is that you will be encouraged and excited about being on the daily journey to the heart of our God. May He richly bless you as you place your hand in His.

Love in Christ,
Cynthia Heald

*Morton T. Kelsey, quoted in *Disciplines for the Inner Life*, ed. Bob Benson and Michael W. Benson (Nashville: Generoux/Nelson, 1989), 134.

How to Use This Journal

T he desire to pursue God is placed within us by God Himself, A. W. Tozer tells us, but our part is to respond by "following hard" after Him.

A Journal for the Journey is a tool to facilitate your pursuit of God. It has been designed as a companion to the book *A Woman's Journey to the Heart of God* by Cynthia Heald. Although you might find it possible to use this journal without the book it accompanies, that is not the way it is intended to be used. Rather, its purpose is to help you move from reading about a woman's journey to the heart of God to taking actual steps on *your* journey to the heart of God. Therefore, you will find it most rewarding to use this as a companion, alongside your reading of Cynthia's book, chapter by chapter.

Use this journal as a place to record your thoughts, wrestle with questions, and apply Cynthia's insights to your own journey with God. The format follows the book's organization. Just as you may read small portions of book chapters at one sitting, so it may be beneficial to complete only portions of each journal segment at any one time. The journal should be a welcome support to your reading, not a performance demand.

Each journal segment contains several questions, exercises, and suggested prayers as springboards for your thoughts and responses. Questions appearing in the text of the book are intended to provoke your thinking while you are reading and to create opportunities to discuss the chapter material with others. The exercises in this journal are intended to help you write down your thoughts, articulate your personal reflections, and lead you into direct conversation with God through prayer. Each journal segment provides a place for "Other

Thoughts" to give you freedom to record any other responses you may have as a result of your reading.

If you have used any of Cynthia Heald's Bible studies, such as *Becoming a Woman of Excellence,* you are familiar with her practice of suggesting specific Scripture passages for memorizing and meditating. *In* A Journal for the Journey, *Scripture memory is suggested but the specific passage is left to your choosing.* You will find many Scriptures from which to choose in each book chapter, or you may prefer to select one from your own reading of God's Word. Space is allotted for you to write out the passage, although you may find it necessary to carry it around with you on a 3" x 5" card for easy reference.

Each time you sit down to write in your *Journal for the Journey,* ask God to be present with you. Seek the guidance of His Holy Spirit to help you be honest in what you say to Him and receptive to what He might be saying to you. Consecrate this tool as a means to moving closer to His heart, and expect His gracious response.

A
Journal
for the
Journey

THE FATHER
AND THE CHILD

The Father spoke:
  Come, child, let us journey together.
  Where shall we go, Father?
  To a distant land, another kingdom.
  So the journey will be long?
  Yes, we must travel every day.
  When will we reach our destination?
  At the end of your days.
  And who will accompany us?
  Joy and Sorrow.
  Must Sorrow travel with us?
  Yes, she is necessary to keep you close to Me.
  But I want only Joy.
  It is only with Sorrow that you will know true Joy.
  What must I bring?
  A willing heart to follow Me.
  What shall I do on the journey?
  There is only one thing that you must do—stay close to
  Me. Let nothing distract you. Always keep your eyes
  on Me.
  And what will I see?
  You will see My glory.
  And what will I know?
  You will know My heart.
The Father stretched out His hand.
The child, knowing the great love her Father had for her,
placed her hand in His and began her journey.

What thoughts do you have as you read this opening conversation
between the Father and the child?

_____

_____

_____

_____

_____

_____

_____

As a prayer to your heavenly Father, write down whatever is on your mind and in your heart as you place your hand in His for the journey ahead.

_____

_____

_____

_____

_____

_____

_____

_____

_____

_____

_____

_____

_____

_____

_____

_____

A Scripture passage for memorizing and meditating:

_____

_____

_____

_____

_____

_____

Preparing for a Lifetime Journey

Once we understand that the journey *begins* with our commitment to travel toward the heart of God, we can be free of the fear of being unprepared. Each day becomes precious because each day is part of the process that takes us nearer to the heart of God.

Describe where you are on your journey (for example, waiting to begin, traveling day by day, postponing your departure until you feel ready, needing guidance for getting under way).

_____

_____

_____

_____

_____

_____

_____

_____

_____

_____

_____

_____

_____

_____

_____

_____

_____

What are the "pulls" on your time and identity that make it hard for you to travel day by day?

_____

_____

_____

_____

_____

_____

_____

_____

_____

_____

_____

_____

_____

_____

_____

_____

_____

_____

_____

_____

_____

_____

_____

_____

In what areas of your life do you especially feel the need to take your Father's outstretched hand?

_____

_____

_____
_____
_____
_____
_____
_____
_____
_____
_____
_____
_____
_____
_____
_____
_____
_____
_____
_____
_____
_____
_____
_____
_____
_____
_____

Other Thoughts

_____
_____
_____
_____
_____
_____

_____
_____
_____
_____
_____
_____
_____
_____
_____
_____
_____
_____
_____
_____
_____
_____
_____
_____

A Scripture passage for memorizing and meditating:

_____
_____
_____
_____

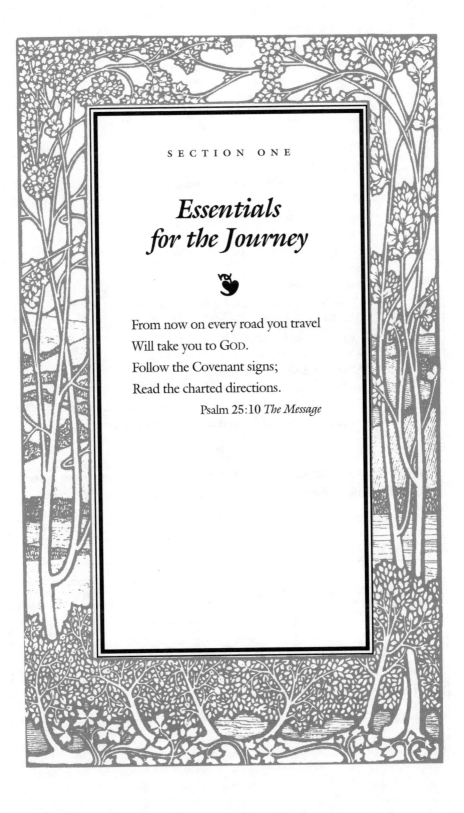

SECTION ONE

Essentials for the Journey

From now on every road you travel
Will take you to GOD.
Follow the Covenant signs;
Read the charted directions.

Psalm 25:10 *The Message*

THE FATHER
AND THE CHILD

The Father spoke:

    Are you ready, My child?

    Yes, but I have nothing to bring except myself.

    You are all I need.

    Surely I must bring something; *I do not feel prepared to travel.*

    Do not concern yourself with preparations. Your journey has already begun.

    But I am fearful.

    There is no need to fear; I will always be with you.

    Will You give me what I need?

    I will provide for you.

    What will You provide?

    All that is essential for your journey.

    And what is essential?

    I will show you along the way. For now, you have what is necessary: the desire to draw close to My heart.

What responses do you have to this conversation between the Father and the child about the essentials for the journey?

_____

_____

_____

_____

_____

_____

In the form of a prayer to your heavenly Father, write down your answer to this question: Are you ready to journey with God in trust, day by day?

_____

_____

A Scripture passage for memorizing and meditating:

11

An
Invitation

Aren't My love and eternal life enough to keep you on your journey? If nothing ever changes and you continue to go through difficulty, you will still have a lifetime of knowing Me and the blessing of living with Me forever.

Describe a turning point in your life when you said yes to God.

_____

_____

_____

_____

_____

_____

_____

_____

_____

_____

_____

_____

_____

_____

_____

_____

_____

_____

_____

_____

_____

_____

_____

_____

_____

_____

_____

_____

In what ways do you identify with the woman at the well?

_____

_____

_____

_____

_____

_____

_____

_____

_____

_____

_____

_____

_____

_____

_____

_____

Have you ever felt loved just for who you are, not for what you can do?
Describe your feelings.

_____

_____

_____
_____
_____
_____
_____
_____
_____
_____
_____
_____
_____
_____
_____
_____
_____
_____
_____

How has your belief in God affected the directions you have taken in life?

_____
_____
_____
_____
_____
_____
_____
_____
_____
_____
_____
_____
_____
_____
_____

_____
_____
_____
_____
_____

In the form of a prayer, say yes to God's invitation to journey with Him day by day.

_____
_____
_____
_____
_____
_____
_____
_____
_____
_____
_____
_____
_____
_____
_____
_____
_____

Other Thoughts

_____
_____
_____
_____
_____
_____

_____

_____

_____

_____

_____

_____

_____

_____

_____

_____

_____

_____

_____

_____

_____

_____

_____

_____

_____

A Scripture passage for memorizing and meditating:

_____

_____

_____

_____

_____

THREE

Relinquish Control

If I choose to believe God, then I must accept His plan and His route for my journey. . . . He is our Father, and He lovingly takes responsibility for our lives. My part is to trust Him by giving up my agenda, saying no to self, and allowing Him to be in control.

Write about an experience in which you learned, or had to learn, to give up control.

_____

_____

_____

_____

_____

_____

_____

_____

_____

_____

_____

_____

_____

_____

_____

_____

_____

_____

_____

_____

_____

_____
_____
_____
_____
_____
_____
_____
_____
_____
_____

List all the reasons it is difficult for you to trust God with whatever route your journey may take.

_____
_____
_____
_____
_____
_____
_____
_____
_____
_____
_____
_____
_____
_____
_____
_____
_____
_____
_____
_____

_____
_____
_____
_____
_____
_____
_____

List all the reasons it can be a joyful experience to trust God with whatever route your journey may take.

_____
_____
_____
_____
_____
_____
_____
_____
_____
_____
_____
_____
_____
_____
_____
_____
_____
_____
_____
_____
_____
_____
_____
_____

_____
_____
_____
_____

Write out a prayer asking God to help you lay aside preoccupation with your inadequacies or shortcomings.

_____
_____
_____
_____
_____
_____
_____
_____
_____
_____
_____
_____
_____
_____
_____
_____
_____
_____

Other Thoughts

_____
_____
_____
_____
_____

_____

_____

_____

_____

_____

_____

_____

_____

_____

_____

_____

_____

_____

_____

_____

_____

_____

_____

A Scripture passage for memorizing and meditating:

_____

_____

_____

_____

_____

Faith for the Unforeseen

To walk by sight is to focus on overpowering hurdles and turn away from a God-directed path. It is to choose a path simply because it seems good and smooth, and then to realize it was the wrong choice. To walk by faith is to allow the Lord to choose the way for us, and then to trust Him with whatever lies ahead.

Are you currently facing any "giants in the land"?

_____

_____

_____

_____

_____

_____

_____

_____

_____

_____

_____

_____

_____

_____

_____

_____

_____

_____

_____

_____

_____

_____

_____

_____

_____

Think of a time when you were surprised by unexpected circumstances.
Was your response one of trusting God or relying on your own insight?

_____

_____

_____

_____

_____

_____

_____

_____

_____

_____

_____

_____

_____

_____

_____

_____

_____

_____

_____

_____

_____

_____

_____

_____

_____

What helps you trust God when you are tempted to worry about what might happen?

_____
_____
_____
_____
_____
_____
_____
_____
_____
_____
_____
_____
_____
_____
_____
_____
_____
_____
_____
_____

In the form of a prayer, tell God your need for deepening your faith in Him for the unforeseen.

_____
_____
_____
_____
_____
_____
_____
_____

_____
_____
_____
_____
_____
_____
_____
_____
_____

Other Thoughts

_____
_____
_____
_____
_____
_____
_____
_____
_____
_____
_____
_____
_____
_____
_____
_____
_____
_____
_____
_____
_____
_____

A Scripture passage for memorizing and meditating:

_____

_____

_____

_____

_____

FIVE

Travel Light

We linger in the lowlands because carrying a heavy load to the mountains is too exhausting. What blessing and glory await us as we move in freedom to the uplands of God! We have a choice. Ultimately, each woman must ask herself, How do I want to journey in this life—plodding along, weighed down with heavy burdens? Or running the race in the freedom of confession, self-control, and forgiveness? Where do I want to spend my life—in the misty valleys or the mysterious hills?

What are the burdens in your life that are weighing you down?

_____
_____
_____
_____
_____
_____
_____
_____
_____
_____
_____
_____
_____
_____
_____
_____

_____
_____
_____

Describe an experience in which you felt a burden lifted from you because you were forgiven.

_____
_____
_____
_____
_____
_____
_____
_____
_____
_____
_____
_____
_____
_____
_____
_____

Describe an experience in which you lifted a burden by extending forgiveness.

_____
_____
_____
_____
_____

_____

_____

_____

_____

_____

_____

_____

_____

_____

_____

_____

_____

Are there any areas in your life right now in which you need to make changes in order to travel light? Write them down in the form of a prayer for wisdom in carrying the changes out.

_____

_____

_____

_____

_____

_____

_____

_____

_____

_____

_____

_____

_____

_____

_____

_____

_____
_____
_____
_____
_____
_____
_____
_____
_____
_____

Other Thoughts

_____
_____
_____
_____
_____
_____
_____
_____
_____
_____
_____
_____
_____
_____
_____
_____
_____
_____
_____
_____

_____
_____
_____
_____
_____

A Scripture passage for memorizing and meditating:

_____
_____
_____
_____
_____

SIX

Fellowship with Our Guide

Your fellowship with God does not necessarily guarantee a good day; it guarantees that you can get through the day to the glory of God.

Reflect on whether or not you view God as a gracious Guide who desires your companionship.

_____

_____

_____

_____

_____

_____

_____

_____

_____

_____

_____

_____

_____

_____

_____

_____

_____

_____

_____

_____

_____

_____

_____

_____

Reread the account of Jesus' visit to the home of Martha and Mary, in
Luke 10:38–42. What do you have in common with Martha?

_____

_____

_____

_____

_____

_____

_____

_____

_____

_____

_____

_____

_____

What do you have in common with Mary?

_____

_____

_____

_____

_____

_____

_____

_____

_____

_____

_____

_____

_____

_____

_____

List as many different ways as you can think of in which you experience a sense of communion with God.

_____

_____

_____

_____

_____

_____

_____

_____

_____

_____

_____

_____

_____

_____

_____

_____

_____

_____

_____

_____

_____

_____

_____

_____

_____

In the form of a prayer, tell God about your desire for fellowship with Him.

_____

_____

_____

_____

_____

_____

_____

_____

_____

_____

_____

_____

_____

_____

_____

_____

_____

_____

_____

_____

Other Thoughts

_____

_____

_____

_____

_____

_____

_____

_____

_____

_____

_____
_____
_____
_____
_____
_____
_____
_____
_____
_____
_____
_____

A Scripture passage for memorizing and meditating:

_____
_____
_____
_____
_____

SEVEN

The Guidebook

The Bible is *the* guidebook to the heart of God. It tells us everything we need to know about how to make this journey. It gives direction; it teaches; it corrects; it trains. It is God's Holy Spirit–breathed book for us to read, study, and meditate on.

In what ways do you use the Bible as your guidebook for your spiritual journey?

_____

_____

_____

_____

_____

_____

_____

_____

_____

_____

_____

_____

_____

_____

_____

_____

_____

_____

_____

_____

How does God use the Scriptures to speak to you?

_____

_____

_____

_____

_____

_____

_____

_____

_____

_____

_____

_____

_____

_____

_____

_____

_____

_____

_____

_____

_____

_____

_____

_____

_____

_____

_____

_____

What is one of your favorite passages in the Bible, and why?

_____

_____

_____
_____
_____
_____
_____
_____
_____
_____
_____
_____
_____
_____
_____
_____
_____
_____
_____
_____
_____
_____
_____
_____
_____
_____

Identify a verse that you especially need at this time in your life. Write it out in the form of a prayer.

_____
_____
_____
_____
_____

Other Thoughts

_____

_____

_____

_____

A Scripture passage for memorizing and meditating:

_____

_____

_____

_____

_____

EIGHT

A Passionate Reverence

I do not fear God out of dread or apprehension of His judgment or apparent sternness. I fear Him by continually standing in awe of His holy and just character. This motivates me to live in a manner that brings Him honor and pleasure.

Have you ever felt a "passionate reverence" for God? Describe your experience.

_____

_____

_____

_____

_____

_____

_____

_____

_____

_____

_____

_____

_____

_____

_____

_____

_____

_____

_____

_____

Describe any ways in which you feel afraid of God.

Describe any ways in which your "fear" of God draws you closer to Him.

_____

_____

_____

_____

_____

_____

_____

_____

_____

_____

_____

_____

_____

_____

_____

_____

_____

_____

_____

_____

_____

_____

_____

_____

_____

_____

Write out a prayer asking God to allow godly fear to set you free from other fears.

_____

_____

Other Thoughts

_____
_____
_____
_____
_____
_____
_____
_____
_____
_____
_____
_____
_____
_____
_____
_____
_____
_____

A Scripture passage for memorizing and meditating:

_____
_____
_____
_____
_____

NINE

Stay on the Path

Obedience is believing that God knows what He is asking, that He gives strength to obey, and that it is always for our good.

How would you define *obedience*?

_____
_____
_____
_____
_____
_____
_____
_____
_____
_____
_____
_____
_____
_____
_____

Why do you think God equates obedience with love for Him?

_____
_____
_____
_____
_____

_____

_____

_____

_____

_____

_____

_____

_____

Describe an experience in which God tested your obedience. How did it strengthen you?

_____

_____

_____

_____

_____

_____

_____

_____

_____

_____

_____

_____

_____

_____

_____

_____

_____

_____

_____

_____

_____

_____

_____

_____

Identify an area of your life in which obeying God tends to be a struggle. In the form of a prayer, tell God about your struggle, and ask for His strength to stay on the path.

_____

_____

_____

_____

_____

_____

_____

_____

_____

_____

_____

_____

_____

_____

_____

_____

_____

_____

_____

_____

_____

_____
_____
_____
_____
_____
_____
_____
_____

Other Thoughts

_____
_____
_____
_____
_____
_____
_____
_____
_____
_____
_____
_____
_____
_____
_____
_____
_____
_____
_____
_____
_____
_____
_____

A Scripture passage for memorizing and meditating:

_____

_____

_____

_____

_____

Righteous Clothing

God does not ask us to be holy because He is a stern taskmaster. He asks us to be holy because He loves us. He knows that sharing in His divine nature is supremely more fulfilling and satisfying than sharing in anything the world offers.

Why do you think C. S. Lewis insisted that holiness is not dull?

_____

_____

_____

_____

_____

_____

_____

_____

_____

_____

_____

_____

_____

_____

_____

_____

_____

_____
_____
_____

Are there any predecisions you need or want to make for traveling on
the highway of holiness? If so, write them out here in preparation for
the moments in which you must make a choice to put on righteous
clothing.

_____
_____
_____
_____
_____
_____
_____
_____
_____
_____
_____
_____
_____
_____
_____
_____
_____
_____
_____
_____
_____
_____
_____
_____
_____

_____
_____
_____
_____
_____
_____
_____
_____
_____
_____
_____
_____
_____
_____

What changes in your life might be necessary to keep your "torch" burning?

_____
_____
_____
_____
_____
_____
_____
_____
_____
_____
_____
_____
_____
_____
_____

_____

_____

_____

_____

_____

_____

_____

_____

_____

_____

If you feel the need for greater sensitivity to your sin, write out a prayer asking God to help you in this area.

_____

_____

_____

_____

_____

_____

_____

_____

_____

_____

_____

_____

_____

_____

_____

_____

_____

Other Thoughts

_____
_____
_____
_____
_____
_____
_____
_____
_____
_____
_____
_____
_____
_____
_____
_____
_____
_____
_____
_____
_____
_____
_____
_____
_____

A Scripture passage for memorizing and meditating:

_____
_____
_____
_____

Wise Traveling Companions

Simple companionship is a wonderful and necessary part of our lives, but a good, wise friend meets us at our point of need and encourages us in the Lord. This ability to strengthen our faith makes *wise* friends indispensable.

Reflect on key individuals throughout your lifetime who have strengthened you in some way on your spiritual journey. Write a brief description of each person and how he or she influenced you.

_____

_____

_____

_____

_____

_____

_____

_____

_____

_____

_____

_____

_____

_____

_____

_____

_____

_____

_____

_____

_____
_____
_____
_____
_____
_____
_____
_____
_____
_____
_____
_____
_____
_____
_____
_____
_____
_____
_____
_____

Write out a job description (qualifications and responsibilities) for a wise traveling companion.

_____
_____
_____
_____
_____
_____
_____
_____

_____
_____
_____
_____
_____
_____
_____
_____
_____
_____
_____
_____
_____
_____
_____
_____

From your experience, list all the ways you can think of in which friends can encourage one another in the Lord.

_____
_____
_____
_____
_____
_____
_____
_____
_____
_____
_____
_____
_____
_____

_____
_____
_____
_____
_____
_____
_____
_____
_____
_____
_____
_____
_____
_____
_____
_____

Write a brief prayer asking God to help you recognize how He can meet your current need for wise friends.

_____
_____
_____
_____
_____
_____
_____
_____
_____
_____
_____
_____
_____
_____
_____
_____

Other Thoughts

_____

_____

_____

_____

_____

_____

_____

_____

_____

_____

_____

_____

_____

_____

_____

_____

_____

_____

_____

_____

_____

_____

_____

_____

_____

A Scripture passage for memorizing and meditating:

_____

_____

_____

_____

TWELVE

Willingness to Endure

When God places us in difficult situations and declines to eliminate the pressure, it is comforting to remember that His grace enables us to keep going when the road is rough. What we consider affliction, the Lord uses to manifest His strength in us.

Describe a situation in which you were glad you persevered.

_____
_____
_____
_____
_____
_____
_____
_____
_____
_____
_____
_____
_____
_____
_____
_____
_____
_____
_____

_____

_____

_____

Can you recall a decisive moment in which God prompted you to sur-
render to His purposes and declare your willingness to follow Him no
matter what happened? Describe the experience.

_____

_____

_____

_____

_____

_____

_____

_____

_____

_____

_____

_____

_____

_____

_____

_____

_____

_____

_____

_____

_____

_____

_____

_____

_____

_____

_____

_____

Reflect on one person from Scripture whose story of endurance encourages you to "press on."

_____

_____

_____

_____

_____

_____

_____

_____

_____

_____

_____

_____

_____

_____

_____

_____

Write out a prayer asking God to cultivate endurance in your life.

_____

_____

_____

_____

_____

_____

_____

_____

_____

_____

_____

_____

_____

_____

_____

Other Thoughts

_____

_____

_____

_____

_____

_____

_____

_____

_____

_____

_____

_____

_____

_____

_____

_____

_____

_____

_____

A Scripture passage for memorizing and meditating:

_____

_____

_____

_____

_____

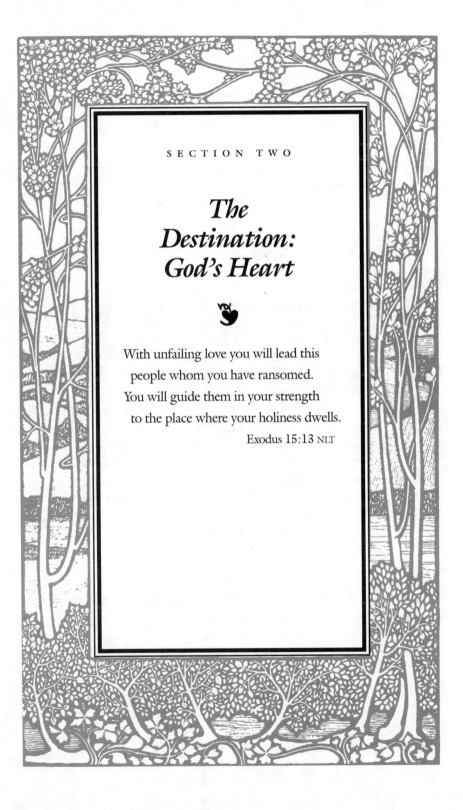

SECTION TWO

The Destination: God's Heart

With unfailing love you will lead this
people whom you have ransomed.
You will guide them in your strength
to the place where your holiness dwells.

Exodus 15:13 NLT

The Father
and the Child

The child spoke:

Father, the journey is harder than I thought it would be. I am weary.

When My Son traveled here, He became weary also.

Why is it so?

Because My kingdom is not yet established.

Am I nearing the destination?

You have come far, but there are still many roads to travel.

Will these roads be any easier?

The closer you come to My heart, the more intensely you will experience My love and understand My ways. You will become more concerned about what is eternal and less concerned about the difficulty of the journey.

Sorrow still walks with me.

She travels with you by My design. She is a carefully chosen tool in My hand to accomplish My will for you.

Sorrow has become more of a friend. I no longer fear her presence. But Joy never leaves me! She has settled deep in my heart. Will she always accompany me?

She will never leave you as long as you keep your hand in Mine and let Me lead you to My heart.

Then she will be with me forever—for I have no other desire than to know Your heart.

What responses do you have to this conversation between the Father and the child as He draws her closer toward His heart?

_____

_____

_____

_____

_____

_____

_____

In the form of a prayer to your heavenly Father, write down your desires and fears regarding a more intimate knowledge of Him.

_____

_____

_____

_____

_____

_____

_____

_____

_____

_____

_____

_____

_____

_____

_____

_____

_____

_____

_____

A Scripture passage for memorizing and meditating:

_____

_____

_____

_____

_____

THIRTEEN

His
Immeasurable Love

Can there be any greater incentive to travel to a destination than the guarantee that when we get there, we will experience complete, unconditional, and eternal love?

How do you know that God loves you, and how much difference does that knowledge make in your life?

_____

_____

_____

_____

_____

_____

_____

_____

_____

_____

_____

_____

_____

_____

_____

_____

_____

_____

_____

_____

_____

_____

_____

_____

_____

_____

_____

_____

Where are you most vulnerable to feeling that God's love is not enough for you?

_____

_____

_____

_____

_____

_____

_____

_____

_____

_____

_____

_____

_____

_____

_____

_____

_____

_____

_____

_____
_____
_____
_____

How has God's loving correction shaped your life?

_____
_____
_____
_____
_____
_____
_____
_____
_____
_____
_____
_____
_____
_____
_____
_____
_____
_____
_____
_____
_____
_____
_____
_____
_____
_____

_____

_____

_____

In the form of a prayer, reflect on the truth that God *chooses* to love you (and, therefore, you can do nothing to earn His love and nothing to lose it).

_____

_____

_____

_____

_____

_____

_____

_____

_____

_____

_____

_____

_____

_____

_____

_____

_____

_____

_____

_____

_____

_____

_____

_____

_____

_____

_____

_____

_____

_____

_____

_____

_____

Other Thoughts

_____

_____

_____

_____

_____

_____

_____

_____

_____

_____

_____

_____

_____

_____

_____

_____

_____

_____

_____

_____

_____

_____

_____

A Scripture passage for memorizing and meditating:

_____

_____

_____

_____

_____

FOURTEEN

His Boundless Grace

The more we learn to receive and depend upon His grace in deepening measure, the less anxious we will be about what the future holds and whether we will have the strength to face it.

How would you define *the grace of God*?

_____

_____

_____

_____

_____

_____

_____

_____

_____

_____

_____

_____

_____

_____

_____

_____

_____

_____

What responses do you have to the account of the woman caught in adultery? (See John 8:1–11.)

_____

_____

_____

_____
_____
_____
_____
_____
_____
_____
_____
_____
_____
_____
_____
_____
_____
_____

Describe an example from the Scriptures that pictures for you the boundless grace of God.

_____
_____
_____
_____
_____
_____
_____
_____
_____
_____
_____
_____
_____
_____
_____
_____

_____

_____

_____

Reflect on one current opportunity you have for reflecting God's grace to others. Describe the difference it can make, or is making, in this circumstance.

_____

_____

_____

_____

_____

_____

_____

_____

_____

_____

_____

_____

_____

_____

_____

_____

_____

_____

_____

_____

_____

_____

_____

_____

Identify a trial God is allowing you to go through. In the form of a prayer, ask Him to use this trial as a way for you to receive His grace and experience more deeply the power of Christ.

_____

_____

_____

_____

_____

_____

_____

_____

_____

_____

_____

_____

_____

_____

_____

_____

_____

_____

_____

_____

_____

_____

_____

_____

Other Thoughts

_____

_____

_____

_____

_____

_____

_____

_____

_____

_____

_____

_____

_____

_____

_____

_____

_____

_____

_____

_____

_____

_____

_____

_____

A Scripture passage for memorizing and meditating:

_____

_____

_____

_____

_____

FIFTEEN

His
Manifold Goodness

My definition of *good* is "anything that makes me happy and my life hassle-free." *God's* definition of *good* is "anything that makes me more like Jesus Christ and brings Him glory."

Reflect on Martha's disappointment when Jesus did not arrive in time to save her brother, Lazarus, from dying. Can you describe a similar experience when you felt that, in essence, God had let you down?

_____

_____

_____

_____

_____

_____

_____

_____

_____

Since that experience of disappointment, how has your understanding of God's goodness changed?

_____

_____

_____

_____

_____

_____

_____

_____

_____

_____

_____

_____

_____

_____

_____

_____

_____

_____

What is one way in which you have seen God's goodness at work in your life through pruning (i.e., cultivating your character rather than manipulating circumstances for your personal happiness)?

_____

_____

_____

_____

_____

_____

_____

_____

_____

_____

_____

_____

_____

_____

_____

_____

_____

_____

_____

_____

_____

_____

_____

_____

_____

_____

_____

What are the specific ways in which you are tempted to doubt God's goodness and to question His care?

_____
_____
_____
_____
_____
_____
_____
_____
_____
_____
_____
_____
_____
_____
_____
_____
_____
_____

In the form of a prayer, tell God where in your life you are most in need of affirming that He works through all circumstances to bring about His good purposes.

_____
_____
_____
_____
_____
_____
_____
_____
_____

_____

_____

_____

_____

_____

_____

_____

_____

_____

_____

_____

_____

_____

_____

_____

_____

_____

_____

_____

_____

Other Thoughts

_____

_____

_____

_____

_____

_____

_____

_____

_____

_____

_____

_____

_____

_____

_____

_____

_____

_____

_____

_____

_____

_____

_____

_____

A Scripture passage for memorizing and meditating:

_____

_____

_____

_____

_____

SIXTEEN

His
Absolute Sovereignty

Although I do not understand the mystery of what God ordains and what He permits, I believe wholeheartedly in the absolute sovereignty of God. I am secure because I know that a loving God is controlling this world.

How would you define *the sovereignty of God*?

_____

_____

_____

_____

_____

_____

_____

_____

_____

_____

_____

_____

_____

_____

_____

_____

_____

_____

_____

_____

What encourages you to trust in the sovereignty of God when you are tempted to feel that He is an idle, unconcerned spectator?

_____

_____

_____

_____

_____

_____

_____

_____

_____

_____

_____

_____

_____

_____

_____

_____

_____

_____

_____

_____

_____

_____

_____

Can you point to a disappointment or setback that you later realized was an important event in God's loving plan for your life? How did it shape your understanding of His sovereignty?

_____

_____

_____

_____

_____

_____

_____

_____

_____

_____

_____

_____

_____

_____

_____

_____

_____

_____

_____

_____

_____

_____

_____

_____

Offer the Lord a prayer of thanksgiving for the way He controls evil and uses it to accomplish His good purposes.

_____

_____

_____

_____

_____

_____
_____
_____
_____
_____
_____
_____
_____
_____
_____
_____
_____
_____

Other Thoughts

_____
_____
_____
_____
_____
_____
_____
_____
_____
_____
_____
_____
_____
_____
_____
_____
_____
_____

_____

_____

_____

_____

A Scripture passage for memorizing and meditating:

_____

_____

_____

_____

_____

SEVENTEEN

His Perfect Will

Our God does not give us a detailed map of what lies ahead and will happen in each of our lives. But He has perfect knowledge of everything we will experience. He has given us the assurance that every step will bring us closer to our ultimate destination, His heart.

In what areas of your life do you particularly struggle with knowing and doing the will of God?

_____
_____
_____
_____
_____
_____
_____
_____
_____
_____
_____
_____
_____
_____
_____
_____
_____
_____
_____

_____

_____

List any attitudes and behaviors in your life that you know work against your ability to understand and obey God's will.

_____

_____

_____

_____

_____

_____

_____

_____

_____

_____

_____

_____

_____

_____

_____

_____

_____

_____

_____

_____

_____

_____

_____

_____

_____

_____

_____

_____

_____

List any attitudes and practices that you know strengthen you to understand and obey God's will.

_____
_____
_____
_____
_____
_____
_____
_____
_____
_____
_____
_____
_____
_____
_____
_____
_____
_____
_____
_____
_____
_____
_____
_____
_____
_____
_____

_____

_____

In the form of a prayer, tell the Lord your specific needs for understanding and obeying His will in the little choices as well as the big decisions.

_____

_____

_____

_____

_____

_____

_____

_____

_____

_____

_____

_____

_____

_____

_____

_____

_____

_____

_____

_____

Other Thoughts

_____

_____

_____
_____
_____
_____
_____
_____
_____
_____
_____
_____
_____
_____
_____
_____
_____
_____
_____
_____
_____
_____
_____
_____

A Scripture passage for memorizing and meditating:

_____
_____
_____
_____

EIGHTEEN

His Incomparable Ways

God knows what He is doing. He has His ways for you, and they are higher and better than what you would settle for on your own. They bring Him glory and accomplish His purposes in your life. He longs to show Himself mighty on your behalf.

List all the differences you can think of between your ways and God's ways for your travel through life.

_____

_____

_____

_____

_____

_____

_____

_____

_____

_____

_____

_____

_____

_____

_____

_____

_____

_____

_____
_____
_____
_____
_____
_____
_____
_____
_____
_____
_____
_____
_____
_____
_____
_____
_____
_____
_____
_____
_____
_____
_____

In what areas of your life are you most tempted to cling to your ways rather than yield to God's ways?

_____
_____
_____
_____
_____
_____
_____
_____

_____
_____
_____
_____
_____
_____
_____
_____
_____
_____
_____
_____
_____
_____
_____
_____
_____
_____
_____
_____

Describe an example from the Scriptures that you feel is a shining affirmation of the statement "God's ways are best."

_____
_____
_____
_____
_____
_____
_____
_____
_____
_____
_____
_____
_____

_____

_____

_____

_____

_____

_____

_____

_____

_____

_____

_____

_____

_____

_____

_____

_____

Has God led you through an encounter with affliction in which you felt the burden tempered by a blessing? If so, write it in the form of a prayer of gratitude.

_____

_____

_____

_____

_____

_____

_____

_____

_____

_____

_____

_____

_____

_____
_____
_____
_____
_____
_____
_____
_____
_____
_____
_____
_____
_____
_____

Other Thoughts

_____
_____
_____
_____
_____
_____
_____
_____
_____
_____
_____
_____
_____
_____
_____
_____
_____
_____

_____

_____

_____

_____

_____

A Scripture passage for memorizing and meditating:

_____

_____

_____

_____

_____

NINETEEN

His Abundant Comfort

How fortunate we are that as our journey takes us through what is fearful and uncertain, we may rely on the comforting presence of our heavenly Father. . . . We are not exempt from trials, but we are never alone in them.

Summarize a few significant experiences in which you received comfort from God. (If appropriate, reflect on whether God "stilled" your soul by delivering you from a trial or by granting you peace in the midst of it.)

_____
_____
_____
_____
_____
_____
_____
_____
_____
_____
_____
_____
_____
_____
_____
_____
_____
_____

_____
_____
_____
_____
_____
_____
_____
_____
_____
_____
_____
_____
_____
_____
_____
_____
_____
_____
_____
_____
_____
_____
_____
_____
_____

Think of a time when you felt that God did not see you in your distress. How did this situation affect your relationship with Him, and what was the outcome?

_____
_____
_____
_____
_____

_____

_____

_____

_____

_____

_____

_____

_____

_____

_____

_____

_____

_____

_____

_____

_____

_____

_____

_____

_____

_____

In what ways has God equipped you to comfort others with the comfort you have received from Him?

_____

_____

_____

_____

_____

_____

_____

_____

_____
_____
_____
_____
_____
_____
_____
_____
_____
_____
_____
_____
_____
_____
_____
_____
_____
_____
_____
_____

Write a prayer asking the Lord to help you discover more fully that He is the God of all comfort.

_____
_____
_____
_____
_____
_____
_____
_____
_____
_____
_____

Other Thoughts

_____

_____

A Scripture passage for memorizing and meditating:

_____

_____

_____

_____

_____

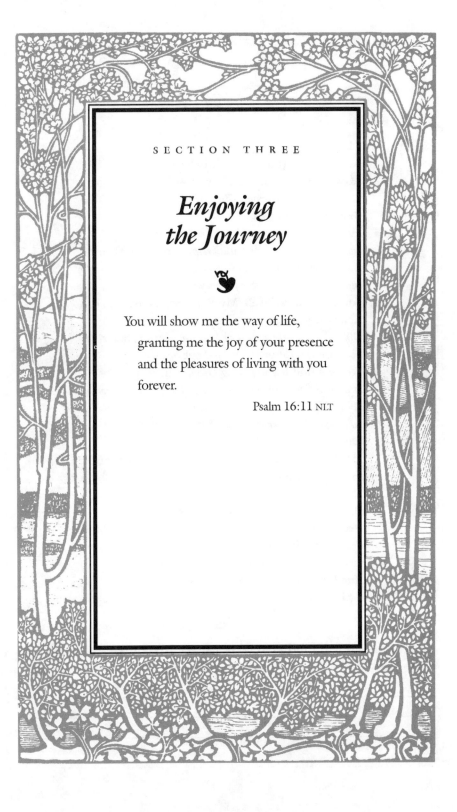

SECTION THREE

Enjoying the Journey

You will show me the way of life,
granting me the joy of your presence
and the pleasures of living with you
forever.

Psalm 16:11 NLT

THE FATHER
AND THE CHILD

The Father spoke:

    And what do you know of My heart?

    I know that Your heart is the only worthy destination.

    How have you learned this truth?

    By walking daily with You.

    How are your companions, Joy and Sorrow?

    Now that I have a better understanding of Your heart, I realize that Sorrow keeps me dependent upon You and Joy enables me to stay on the journey.

    You have learned well, My child. So you wish to continue the journey?

    Oh, Father, I only pray that I remain faithful and obedient. I want no other journey—I seek no other Joy.

    You will find Joy in loving and serving others.

    It is hard for me to love and serve. How can I do it with Joy?

    By taking My yoke and learning of Me.

    As long as I am yoked to You, Father, I know I can do anything.

    Hold My hand tightly, My child. For this part of the journey, you must receive My rest and learn to live for all that is eternal.

    Why must I hold Your hand tightly?

    Because I am ready to place you as a laborer in My harvest, and I do not want you to be so busy in your service that you loosen your grip or let go.

    And how do I labor in Your harvest?

    By bringing Me glory.

What are your thoughts in response to this conversation between the Father and the child as they reflect on what she has learned?

_____

_____

_____

_____

_____

_____

_____

Write out a prayer to your heavenly Father as a reflection on insights
He has given you in recent days or weeks.

_____

_____

_____

_____

_____

_____

_____

_____

_____

_____

_____

_____

_____

_____

_____

_____

_____

A Scripture passage for memorizing and meditating:

_____

_____

_____

_____

TWENTY

Bearing His Fruit

A branch must stay connected to the Vine if it is to bear fruit. And that is *all* the branch has to do! As we stay joined to the Lord, His life will begin to flow through us. In that living union, our inner *being* gives rise to our *doing*.

Write down the first five or six examples that come to mind when you think of Christians bearing fruit.

_____

_____

_____

_____

_____

_____

_____

_____

_____

_____

_____

_____

_____

_____

_____

_____

_____

_____

_____

_____

_____

_____

What attitudes or behaviors are you cultivating that strengthen you to live as a branch connected to the Vine?

_____

_____

_____

_____

_____

_____

_____

_____

_____

_____

_____

_____

_____

_____

_____

_____

_____

_____

_____

What attitudes or behaviors weaken your ability to stay connected to the Vine?

_____

_____

_____

_____

_____

_____

_____

_____

_____

———————————————
———————————————
———————————————
———————————————
———————————————
———————————————
———————————————
———————————————

Make a list of your potential opportunities, in the course of a typical week, for bearing fruit in acts of love for others. Then write out a brief prayer asking God to make you alert to these opportunities.

———————————————
———————————————
———————————————
———————————————
———————————————
———————————————
———————————————
———————————————
———————————————
———————————————
———————————————
———————————————
———————————————
———————————————
———————————————
———————————————
———————————————

Other Thoughts

_____

_____

_____

_____

_____

_____

_____

_____

_____

_____

_____

A Scripture passage for memorizing and meditating:

_____

_____

_____

_____

TWENTY-ONE

Experiencing His Rest

Rest, refreshment, and *renewal* are healing words. God wants to make them a reality in your life.

What comes to mind when you reflect on the words *rest, refreshment,* and *renewal*?

_____

_____

_____

_____

_____

_____

_____

_____

_____

_____

_____

_____

_____

_____

_____

_____

_____

_____

_____

_____

_____

_____

_____
_____
_____
_____
_____
_____
_____
_____
_____
_____
_____
_____
_____
_____
_____
_____
_____
_____
_____
_____
_____
_____

List all of the places and ways in which you have experienced rest and renewal in recent weeks and months, or in the past year.

_____
_____
_____
_____
_____
_____
_____
_____
_____
_____

_____
_____
_____
_____
_____
_____
_____
_____
_____
_____
_____
_____
_____
_____
_____
_____
_____
_____

In what respects would you describe Christ's "yoke" as a restful one?

_____
_____
_____
_____
_____
_____
_____
_____
_____
_____
_____
_____
_____
_____

_____
_____
_____
_____
_____

What fatigue or anxiety are you carrying that might be eased by a deeper experience of God's rest?

_____
_____
_____
_____
_____
_____
_____
_____
_____
_____
_____
_____
_____
_____
_____
_____
_____
_____
_____
_____
_____
_____
_____
_____
_____

_____

_____

In the form of a prayer, write a personal RSVP to Christ's invitation in Matthew 11:28–30.

_____

_____

_____

_____

_____

_____

_____

_____

_____

_____

_____

_____

_____

_____

_____

_____

_____

_____

Other Thoughts

_____

_____

_____

_____

_____

_____

_____

_____
_____
_____
_____
_____
_____
_____
_____
_____
_____
_____
_____
_____
_____
_____
_____
_____

A Scripture passage for memorizing and meditating:

_____
_____
_____
_____
_____

TWENTY-TWO

Living for the Eternal

To understand the difference between living *for* heaven and demanding that life here on earth *be like* heaven is an important lesson in learning to live for the eternal.

How would you describe the difference between living for the eternal (i.e., what ultimately matters) and living for the temporal (i.e., what matters in the here and now)?

_____

_____

_____

_____

_____

_____

_____

_____

_____

_____

_____

_____

_____

_____

_____

_____

_____

_____

_____

_____

_____

_____

_____

_____

_____

_____

_____

_____

_____

_____

_____

Take some time to reflect on one or two key areas of your life—for example, nurturing your spiritual life; family commitments; relationships; work or vocation issues; material possessions; use of time; or use of money. To what extent do your priorities in these areas reflect eternal versus temporal perspectives?

_____

_____

_____

_____

_____

_____

_____

_____

_____

_____

_____

_____

_____

_____

_____

_____

_____
_____
_____

What do you find is the greatest motivator to living for what is eternal?

_____
_____
_____
_____
_____
_____
_____
_____
_____
_____
_____
_____
_____
_____

In the form of a prayer, thank God for preparing an eternity of the very best He has to offer, and ask Him to focus your desires on Him above all else.

_____
_____
_____
_____
_____
_____
_____
_____
_____
_____

Other Thoughts

_____

_____

_____

_____

_____

_____

_____

_____

_____

_____

A Scripture passage for memorizing and meditating:

_____

_____

_____

_____

TWENTY-THREE

Bringing God Glory

The difference between the Pharisee and the true disciple is
that the Pharisee serves in order to be noticed; the true
disciple serves in order that God might be noticed.

**Identify an area of your life in which you struggle with seeking to be
noticed instead of seeking only to bring God glory. Write down how
your attitudes and behaviors differ when your motivation is that of the
Pharisee versus that of the true disciple.**

When I am more like the Pharisee, I . . .

_____

_____

_____

_____

_____

_____

_____

_____

_____

_____

_____

_____

_____

_____

_____

_____

When I am more like the true disciple, I . . .

_____

_____

_____

_____

_____

_____

_____

_____

_____

_____

_____

_____

_____

_____

Reflect on any tendencies you might have to glorify another person in place of God. What signals might indicate when you are stepping across the line from legitimate cherishing to sinful idolizing?

_____

_____

_____

_____

_____

_____

_____

_____

_____

_____

_____

_____

_____

_____

_____

_____
_____
_____
_____
_____
_____
_____
_____
_____
_____
_____
_____

Describe a significant experience in which you have tasted the joy of giving up self-seeking so that God alone might be glorified.

_____
_____
_____
_____
_____
_____
_____
_____
_____
_____
_____
_____
_____
_____
_____
_____
_____
_____

_____
_____
_____
_____
_____
_____
_____
_____
_____

Write a brief prayer asking God to teach you how to focus your life more completely on glorifying Him.

_____
_____
_____
_____
_____
_____
_____
_____
_____
_____
_____
_____

Other Thoughts

_____
_____
_____
_____
_____

A Scripture passage for memorizing and meditating:

The Father
and the Child

The child spoke:

I'm nearing the end of my journey, aren't I, Father?

Yes, My child, but there are still a few more roads to travel.

It has been a good journey. Thank You for holding my hand.

Have you lacked for anything?

No, nothing. I must confess I was skeptical that all I needed to take on the journey was a willing heart. I didn't realize then that when You have my heart, You are all I ever need or want.

What have you learned from your travels?

I've learned that being a woman who pleases You has nothing to do with my family, my friends, or my circumstances, but everything to do with how much I love You and how deeply I abide in You.

How would you describe your journey?

As a journey that frees me to become all You created me to be—as a journey of great inner Joy.

What have you learned about Joy?

Joy has always been deep in my heart, but she is quiet. I've learned that I must be still to hear her; otherwise, I listen to louder voices that silence hers.

How has Joy served you?

She has faithfully been with me in all of my journey—my trials, my suffering, my obedience, and my serving. I understand now that she always accompanies Sorrow—but her most precious gift to me is her tears as I experience Your presence.

How has Sorrow helped you?

Father, I know I said in the beginning that I didn't want Sorrow to go with me, but she has taught me much. Without her, I would never have wept over my sin. Whenever I was deeply hurt or grieving, she took me straight to Your heart. Without her, I would not have known how others felt. I would not have known how to love or serve them. And as